Contents

Sail a longship

Around 1,200 years ago bands of fighters sailed across to Britain from Norway, Denmark and Sweden. We call them the Vikings. Eventually they settled in some parts of Britain.

Sea-going slavers

The first Vikings arrived in 793 CE. They stole valuables and people, who they took home and sold as slaves. They attacked villages, towns and churches, and killed anyone who tried to stop them. The people who lived in Britain at this time were Christian but the early Viking pirates were pagan. They believed in their own gods and goddesses, so they didn't care about destroying churches.

A star journey

The raiders sailed across in long narrow boats called longships, rowing their boat or rigging up a square sail to catch the wind. They found their way using their knowledge of the sun, stars and the sea. They brought dried, salted meat and fish to eat on the journey to Britain, which took a few days.

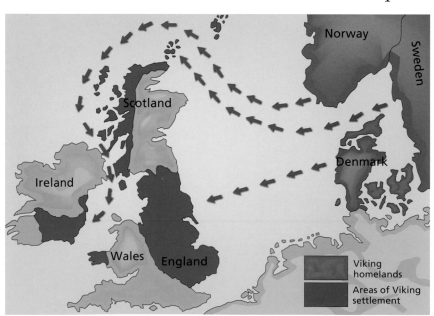

Norway

Sweden

Scotland

Denmark

Ireland

Wales   England

Viking homelands

Areas of Viking settlement

◀ This map shows the routes that Vikings took to reach Britain.

If you lived in Viking times...

If you lived on the coast of Ireland, Scotland or England at this time, the sight of an approaching Viking longship would have filled you with terror! This photo shows a modern reconstruction.

A dragon onboard

Longships were strong, reliable ships that could be sailed up rivers and across seas and oceans. The prow (front) of a longship was carved in the shape of a dragon, probably to impress and scare anyone who saw it. Some ships had carved sides painted in colours such as black, red, yellow and brown.

Look!

At a Viking village called Jarlshof in Shetland, Scotland (see p12), doodles of boats have been found scratched onto pieces of slate which date from Viking times.

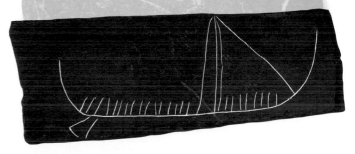

Attack!

The early Vikings did not write down their history but we know something about their attacks because British monks wrote about what happened.

Treasure grabbing

British monks lived in religious communities called monasteries at the time, where they kept sacred treasures such as fine gold crosses and precious books decorated with jewels. In 793 the Vikings launched a raid on a famous monastery at Lindisfarne in Northumberland, murdering monks and stealing treasures. They ripped up precious books to steal the jewels from their covers.

Look

The Lindisfarne Priory Stone is a 9th century carving that once marked a grave at the monastery. It shows Vikings waving their weapons.

Summer trouble

The Vikings attacked in spring and summer, when the weather was good for sailing. They raided towns they could reach by boat, such as London, Southampton and Canterbury, as well as monasteries around the country. They may have set up pirate bases on the coast of Ireland and the Hebrides in Scotland, launching their attacks and then escaping back to base with their haul.

Iron men

The Viking raiders were armed with iron swords, axes and spears. They carried wooden shields painted in different colours, and in the middle of the shield there was a round iron piece called a boss, which would have been useful for pushing an enemy over. The wealthiest warriors probably wore iron helmets but the poorer ones may have worn leather caps.

These Viking re-enactors are wearing replica helmets and are carrying replica weapons. ▼

If you lived in Viking times...

If you had been born in Britain you would not have understood the Viking raiders. They spoke a language from Scandinavia called Old Norse.

Join an army

In 865 an extra-large Viking war band arrived in England from Denmark. They landed in eastern England and stayed, gradually conquering more land. They fought the local English Christian people, who we call the Anglo-Saxons.

▲ Re-enactors recreate the arrival of the Great Army.

If you lived in Viking times...

If you were one of the Great Army you lived a tough life of fighting, travelling and camping. Evidence from the skeletons found at Repton (see p9) suggests that these Vikings were more likely to die from disease than wounds.

Taking over

We call this war band the Great Army. We know that it moved around England, fighting in summer and making camp in winter. By 879–80 its leaders had conquered much of northern and eastern England, including the important town of York. The army set up winter camps in different spots, including London, Exeter, Nottingham and Repton in Derbyshire.

Riverside campside

At Repton we know that the Great Army camped by a river around an old church. Here they buried some of their dead, including warriors with swords and axes, some of whom had suffered battle wounds. The things they left behind are on display at Derby Museum, including the remains of a skull that may have been smashed in during a battle.

King Olaf the White

Vikings were conquering parts of Scotland, too. In 870–71 the Viking King of Dublin, Olaf the White, arrived to attack the Britons who ruled Strathclyde. He besieged their fortress on the rock of Dumbarton and they held out bravely for four months until their well ran dry. Olaf captured many of them to sell as slaves in Ireland.

9

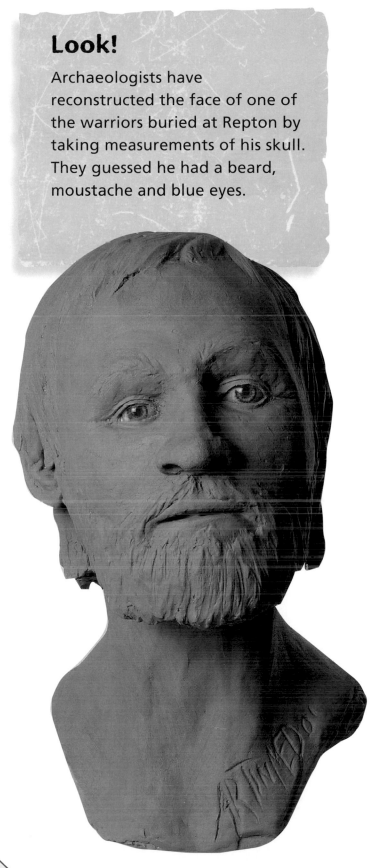

Look!

Archaeologists have reconstructed the face of one of the warriors buried at Repton by taking measurements of his skull. They guessed he had a beard, moustache and blue eyes.

Find the Vikings

The Viking leaders took over land in Britain and Ireland and their followers settled there, farming or living in towns.

A new home

The Vikings settled in Scotland, Ireland, the Isle of Man and in the Danelaw, the name for the areas of England they controlled – in the south, east and north. They brought their Scandinavian customs, such as ways of dressing and speaking, but they also mixed with local people and learnt new ways of living. Over time, they gradually became Christian like the local people.

The handle of this Viking knife is made of animal bone. ▼

Place names

Vikings named the places where they settled, or slightly changed old place names they heard. If you see these place-name endings, you can be pretty

Look!

Everyday Viking objects are sometimes found in places where Vikings once lived. We can tell the knife (below) is Viking because knives like this have been found in Scandinavia, although this one was found in East Anglia. It is over 1,000 years old.

certain that Viking settlers once lived there:

-thwaite – meaning a woodland clearing;
-thorpe – a small settlement;
-by – a farm or a village;
-kirk – a church;
-toft – a building.

That's a Viking name!

Do you know anyone called Eric, Erica, Harold, Freya, Astrid or Brenda? It's thought that these modern names were in use by the Vikings and have come down to us from those times. We know that the Vikings often used their own names to create place names, too. For instance, Slingsby in Yorkshire is where a Viking called Sleng lived with his family.

Thwaite is a village in North Yorkshire that was once part of the Danelaw, hence its Viking place name. ▼

If you lived in Viking times...

There was no King of Britain when the Vikings came. Different warlords were in control of areas of land, and if you were an ordinary person you would have to obey whoever conquered your region.

THWAITE

Stay on a farm

Many Viking families spent their days farming small strips of land. They ate the grain they grew and the animals they raised.

Near neighbours

You can see the remains of a Viking farming village at Jarlshof on the mainland of Shetland. It had several homes where a few families lived together as neighbours. Between them they shared a bakery for baking their loaves and a smithy for making metal tools. They even had a bath-house. Vikings were known for being clean, washing regularly and combing their hair (writers said they were cleaner than Anglo-Saxons!).

Inside a house

Each family lived in a long narrow building called a longhouse. They lived together in one long space, sitting and sleeping on benches covered with animal skins. In the middle of the house there was a fire for cooking and heating, and in the evening the family sat together

Look!

One of the Viking objects found at Jarlshof was a board game. The board was scratched out on a piece of slate and the pieces were pebbles. We can only guess at the rules, though.

▲ In this reconstruction of a longhouse you can see a bench covered with animal skins and woven cloth.

around the fire, sewing clothes, mending tools, telling stories or playing games.

Farm food

We know that the Viking farmers at Jarlshof grew wheat and rye to make bread, barley to make beer, and oats to make porridge. They made butter and cheese, grew vegetables and caught fish to eat. They also kept sheep, cattle and pigs. Archaeologists have excavated rubbish pits to find out what Vikings ate.

If you lived in Viking times...

Children did not go to school in Viking times. They helped their parents with farm work as soon as they were strong enough.

Go to town

York was one of most important Viking towns. When the Vikings conquered it they renamed it Jorvik because they couldn't pronounce its old name, Eoforwic.

Walk through Jorvik

Viking Jorvik was made up of muddy streets lined with small thatched buildings. Craftspeople lived and work there, making pottery, woodwork, leather, glass and carved bone objects. You might have used a small silver coin to buy goods.

In York you can visit a reconstruction of Viking streets at the Jorvik Viking Centre. ▼

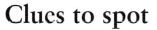

Look!

All sorts of Viking objects have been discovered in York – including the leather shoes shown here. Somebody left them in the backyard behind a Viking workshop long ago.

Clues to spot

The Vikings have left behind some clues that show that they once ruled York. Some streets still have the name 'gate', from the Old Norse word *gata*, meaning street. The name of one of its streets, Coppergate, means 'the street of the cup makers'. We know that Viking craftspeople made wooden cups and bowls in workshops here because of wooden remains they left behind.

Meet some people

The ordinary people of Jorvik were not dressed as warriors. The men wore woollen trousers and a tunic (long shirt) tied round with a leather belt. The women wore a long underdress with a woollen overdress on top. Both the men and women had big brooches pinned to their shoulders to keep their clothes in place. Buttons hadn't been invented yet!

If you lived in Viking times...

You would have worn clothes that were dyed different colours using plants gathered in the countryside. You wouldn't have owned many clothes unless you were very rich.

15

Bury a Viking

When the Vikings first arrived in Britain they were pagan. They believed in lots of gods and goddesses, not the Christian God of the Bible.

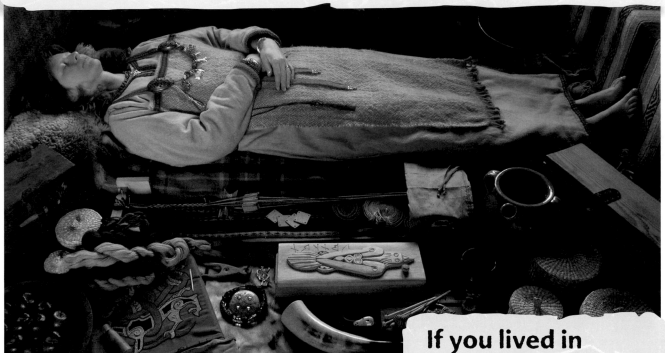

▲ This recreation of a Viking boat burial shows a model of a woman along with objects she might have been buried with.

Taking it with you

Pagan Vikings believed that dead people went on a journey to a new life in a different world. They buried their dead with objects that they might need. Warriors needed swords and shields, and ordinary people needed tools.

If you lived in Viking times...

Pagan Vikings believed that their gods influenced what happened to them. For instance, if you were a warrior you might have worn a pendant in the shape of the hammer that belonged to the war god Thor, to bring you luck in battle. There is one at the top of this page.

Women were buried with jewellery such as brooches and bead necklaces, and children were often buried with their wooden toys.

Buried by boat

A few Viking leaders were buried in large wooden boats, probably to sail them to their new life along with all the things they needed. A boat burial was discovered at Balladoole, on the Isle of Man, with the body of a man inside. He had been buried with belongings including a sword, shield and cauldron (a big cooking pot). The wood of the boat had rotted away by the time it was found, though.

Magical worlds

The pagan Vikings believed that their gods lived in a kingdom in the sky called Asgard, connected to the Earth by a rainbow bridge. In Asgard there was a hall called Valhalla, where warriors who died in battle went for an afterlife of fun and feasting. Beneath the Earth there was a misty chilly world called Nifelheim, the home of the dead, and there were other worlds, too, where giants, dwarves and elves lived.

Look!

This whalebone board (right), carved with two dragons, came from a Viking boat burial at Scar, Orkney. Three people – a man, an older lady and a child – were buried in the boat. Nobody knows why they all died at the same time, or what the board was used for.

Come to a party

Vikings held feasts to celebrate victories, festivals and special events such as weddings. They gathered together to eat, drink and have fun.

Warrior's dinner

Viking leaders and their warriors based themselves in a big thatched hall where they all ate and slept. They held feasts after a battle or a hunt, eating lots of roast meats and drinking beer or mead (an alcoholic drink made from honey).

A reconstruction of a Viking hall. Warriors sat and slept on the long benches. ▼

If you lived in Viking times...

Like us, the Vikings would have looked forward to special days such as weddings, when families would gather to celebrate. At Viking weddings we know that there was a special meal and the bride and groom shared a drink of honey mead.

Re-enactors enjoy a drink from a drinking horn. ▶

Musicians and storytellers, called skalds, entertained the feasters, who also enjoyed wrestling contests.

On the menu

If you lived in Viking times in Britain you ate honey, but you would never have tasted sugar. It hadn't arrived in Europe yet. You ate a lot of carrots and onions, but potatoes, tomatoes and sweetcorn had not yet been discovered by Europeans. You would never have seen tropical fruits such as bananas or pineapples. You ate meals using a spoon and a knife, but forks hadn't been invented yet.

Look!

Viking warriors drank from a drinking horn made from the horn of a cow. It's not true that Vikings had cow horns fitted to their helmets, though.

Fantastic festivals

Everyone feasted at special festival times through the Viking year. From 20 December to the end of the year, there were 12 days of feasting, called Jul. These celebrated the coming of the new year, when the god Odin was believed to ride across the sky on his eight-legged horse, Sleipnir. In spring everyone celebrated the festival of the goddess Eostre, who had rabbits and eggs as her symbols. Later these festivals turned into the Christian celebrations of Christmas and Easter.

Hear a story

Viking people did not have books to read, but they loved hearing magical myths and legends of brave fighting heroes.

Sigurd's stone

Viking stories were told in sagas – long poems full of action and excitement. Scenes from the sagas are sometimes found on stone carvings made in Britain in Viking times. The carving shown here comes from Kirk Bradden on the Isle of Man, and it shows a hero called Sigurd, who starred in a saga about his adventures.

Roasting a dragon

Sigurd killed a dragon called Fafni, and then roasted its heart. The rings on the carving are pieces of the heart that Sigurd is cooking over a

◀ On the Sigurd Slab you can see Sigurd roasting three rings of dragon heart over a fire.

Look!

The comb case shown below was found in Lincoln. It is marked with runes that say: *Thorfast made a good comb.* Perhaps the Viking comb maker Thorfast scratched this on his comb case as an advert!

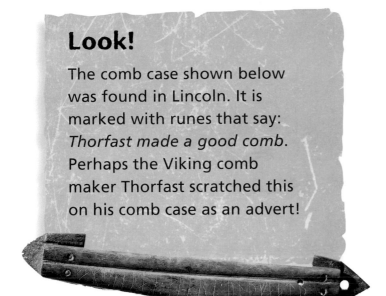

fire. As he cooked, Sigurd burnt his fingers and when he sucked them he tasted dragon's blood, which gave him super-powers. He found he could understand the language of the birds, which later helped him to escape his enemies.

Picture writing

The Vikings did write a few things down, using picture symbols called runes as letters. An owner might scratch his name in runes on something belonging to him, and runes were carved on memorial stones to remember people who had died. They were sometimes used to write down magic spells, too, such as a curse on someone or a cure for illness.

If you lived in Viking times...

If you were a good poet and teller of tales you might one day become a skald (a storyteller) for an important Viking leader, telling stories to him and his warriors in their great feasting hall.

◄ Viking storytellers learnt their stories by listening to other storytellers.

Make some laws

In the areas of Britain controlled by the Vikings people followed Viking laws. The way they organised themselves still affects the way we make laws and judge crimes today.

Men meet up

Every summer Vikings from across a region met up in one spot at a gathering called a Thing. Here they could swap news, decide on new laws and judge crimes or arguments between people. Any Viking freeman (someone who was not a slave) could have his say at the discussions but women could not. Dingwall in Scotland and Tingwall in Shetland get their names because they were once places where a Viking Thing was held.

Look!

The Houses of Parliament (shown below with Viking re-enactors sailing past) has Viking connections. Members of Parliament (MPs) meet up to pass laws, and some of them may be elected as MPs in a contest called a by-election. The word *by* is the Old Norse word for town.

If you lived in Viking times...

A Thing meeting was a good place for families to meet up and arrange marriages. If you were a woman you probably wouldn't get much of a say on who you married. The family heads would probably organise it for you at the Thing, acted out here by re-enactors.

Midsummer mound

On the Isle of Man the Vikings met up on a grassy mound called the Tynwald to make laws. Once every year the Tynwald still meets on the same mound to pass island laws, making it one of the world's oldest parliaments. The Tynwald didn't always run smoothly, though. Sometimes the discussions ended in a violent battle between groups of opposing Vikings.

Guilty?

Crimes were judged by a jury (a group of people) at a Thing, and we still use similar juries to judge crimes in court today. If somebody was found guilty of a crime in Viking times they might be fined or they could be banished as an outlaw. That meant they had to leave the area forever, and anybody was allowed to kill them if they caught them.

Find a treasure

Several buried hoards of treasure have been found around Viking Britain, and new ones are still being discovered!

Secret silver

The hoards often include coins, jewellery and silver arm rings that were once exchanged as money. Sometimes the metal objects have been cut up into pieces called 'hacksilver'. The pieces were weighed and used as money instead of coins. One of the biggest hoards ever found

If you lived in Viking times...

You would have owned lots of treasure if you were an important warrior or leader. Sometimes Viking warlords forced their enemies to pay them not to attack, and gathered wealth that way.

was the Cuerdale Hoard in Lancashire (shown below left). It contained more than 8,600 silver objects buried by Vikings.

Mystery money

We don't know why Vikings buried treasure and never came back to get it. Perhaps they hid it before they went to battle, but then got killed, or they might have buried it as an offering to their gods. From the dates on coins found in the Cuerdale treasure we can tell it was buried at a time when different groups of Vikings were fighting each other. Perhaps the treasure belonged to a Viking band fighting at the time, and was hidden so it would be ready to use when they needed it.

Viking style

The objects found in Viking hoards and graves are often decorated in a way that shows they were made by Viking craftspeople. They have pictures of monsters and animals wound around each other, and lines of twisting patterns. You can see the style on jewellery, weapons and stone carvings.

Look!

The centre part of the Pitney Brooch, shown above, shows Viking-style animals winding around each other. Can you see a snake with bulging eyes? It is biting a mystery monster that is biting its own tail.

Go to church

When the Vikings became Christian they built churches in the areas where they lived. Their word for a church was *kirkja*, and in Scotland churches are often still called kirks.

Telltale stones

In churches that were built in Viking areas you can sometimes still see stone carvings decorated with Viking patterns and animals. The picture above shows the top of a Viking grave from Heysham churchyard in

▲ Can you see Sigurd escaping from magic wolves on the side of the gravestone?

Lancashire. It has carved bear heads on either end. On this side of the stone the carving shows the hero Sigurd (p20) escaping from wolves.

Saint Magnus the Viking

Many Christian people worship saints – holy people who have died. The Vikings on Orkney created their own Viking saint called Saint Magnus. The story goes that as the young son of a Viking warrior, Magnus refused to fight in raids. When he grew up he was killed by his enemies, but then miracles began to happen around his tomb.

Saint Olaf the warrior

Another Viking warrior saint, Saint Olaf, has churches named after him in London and the north of England. He was a king of Norway and it is said that he converted his countrymen to Christianity. During his life he was a violent fighter who attacked London and was himself killed by an enemy axe. Later it was claimed he performed holy deeds and miracles.

Follow the Vikings

The Vikings had a big effect on the way we live in Britain, especially in the north and east. Their descendants continued to rule parts of the country for many centuries.

Attacking again

One thousand years ago southern Britain was not a peaceful country to live in! The Anglo-Saxons and the local Vikings continued to fight each other, and Danish Vikings began sailing over to attack the country again, demanding money to go away. They besieged and burnt down London several times, and at the Museum of London you can see some of the weapons they used. Danish axes and spears have been found in the River Thames.

Vikings rule the south

From 1016 to 1035 the whole of southern Britain was ruled by Viking King Cnut, who was the King of Denmark and Norway, too. Then in 1066 William the Conqueror invaded England

Look!

This coin shows King Cnut wearing a helmet. It was made during the time Cnut ruled England. He ruled Denmark and Norway, too.

▲ The shoreline of Orkney. Vikings ruled here for centuries.

from France and was crowned king. He and his followers were descended from the Vikings, and the modern British royal family are related to William. We could say that the Vikings still rule!

Vikings rule up north
In Scotland and the Isle of Man Vikings ruled for centuries. The Isle of Man was Norwegian until 1266 and the Shetland Isles and Orkney were Danish

until the 1400s. Roughly 30 per cent of the people who live in Orkney today have ancestors from Scandinavia, and it's thought that, overall, about a million people in Britain today are descended from the Vikings who settled in Britain.

Glossary

Anglo-Saxons People who settled in England before the Vikings came.

Asgard The heavenly home of Viking gods and goddesses, linked to Earth by a rainbow bridge.

Boss A round metal knob in the middle of a shield.

Cauldron A large metal cooking pot made to hang over a fire.

Christian Someone who follows the teachings of the Holy Bible.

Freeman Someone who owned land and was not a slave.

Great Army A big group of Vikings who came over to Britain in 865 CE and stayed, gradually conquering part of the country.

Hoard A hidden pile of treasure.

Jorvik The Viking name for the town of York.

Jul A Viking winter festival held at the same time of year as we now celebrate Christmas.

Longhouse A long building where Viking families lived in one inside space.

Longship A long narrow Viking seaboat powered by sails or rowers.

Mead An alcoholic drink made from honey.

Nifelheim A misty cold land where the dead were said to live.

Odin The most important Viking god. He was god of war, the sky, death and wisdom.

Old Norse The language spoken by the Vikings who arrived in Britain.

Pagan Someone who believes in many gods and goddesses, not the God of the Holy Bible.

Runes Viking picture symbols.

Saga A story spoken out loud.

Scandinavian From Scandinavia, the region of the world that includes Denmark, Norway, Sweden and Finland.

Skald A Viking storyteller.

Thing A gathering of Vikings to decide new laws and judge crimes.

Valhalla A heavenly feasting hall for warriors who died in battle.

Further information

Weblinks

http://www.bbc.co.uk/scotland/history/articles/kingdom_of_the_britons/
Read the story of Olaf the White's capture of the rock of Dumbarton.

http://kepn.nottingham.ac.uk/
Does your home town have a Viking name? Discover what it means.

http://thevikingworld.pbworks.com/w/page/4842629/Traditional%20Viking%20
Foods Try cooking a Viking-style recipe such as bread, soup, stew or pancakes.

http://jorvik-viking-centre.co.uk
Discover Viking York and see some of the amazing Viking objects found there.

Note to parents and teachers: Every effort has been made by the Publishers to ensure that the web sites in this book are suitable for children, that they are of the highest educational value, and that they contain no inappropriate or offensive material. However, because of the nature of the Internet, it is impossible to guarantee that the contents of these sites will not be altered. We strongly advise that Internet access is supervised by a responsible adult.

Timeline

793 CE Vikings raid Lindisfarne Abbey in Northumberland.

794 Vikings attack Scotland.

795 Vikings attack Ireland.

866 The Vikings capture the town of York.

878 Anglo-Saxon King Alfred defeats a Viking attack on his kingdom of Wessex.

886 England is divided by a treaty, with the Vikings ruling the Danelaw area and the King of Wessex ruling the rest.

927 Athelstan of Wessex defeats a big force of Vikings and Scots to become the King of all Britain.

954 The last Viking King of York, Eric Bloodaxe, is defeated.

994 The Vikings besiege London.

1013 Swein Forkbeard from Denmark drives out Anglo-Saxon King Aethelred the Unready and takes control of England, but dies before he is crowned.

1014 Forkbeard's son Cnut is crowned and becomes the first Scandinavian to rule England. He rules Denmark too.

1066 William of Normandy conquers England. He is of Viking descent.

Index